A HISTORY OF THE
UNITED STATES

BOOK THREE:
The Growth of the United States

Dr. Marilyn Thypin
Lynne Glasner

Consultant

Dr. James P. Shenton
Dept. of History
Columbia University

Entry Publishing Co., Inc.
New York

Acknowledgments

The photographs included in this text appear courtesy
of the following:

Library of Congress—pages 3, 5, 7, 9, 12, 13, 14, 20, 23,
28, 30, 32, 35, 36, 40, 43, 45, 47, 49, 50, 51, 53, 62, 64,
65, 67, 72, 77, 78, 88.

The National Archives—page 58.

Maps by Shelley Dell
Cover design by Marjorie Waxman
Edited by Jane Lebow
Photo research by Shirley L. Green

ISBN 0-941342-00-X (series)
    0-941342-03-4 (Book Three)

Published by Entry Publishing Co., Inc.
27 West 96th Street, New York, New York, 10025

Printed in the United States of America
    9   8   7   6   5   4   3

CONTENTS

CHAPTER 1

Life in the North

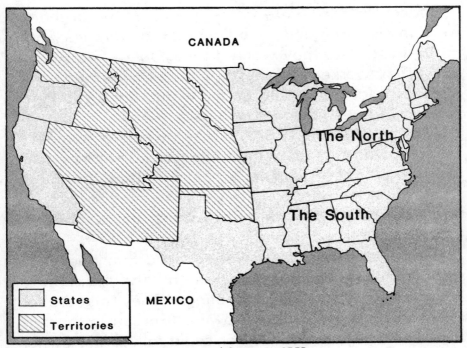

The United States in 1859

The United States in the 1850s

The North is the states in the northeast part of the United States. People from the North are called northerners. Many northerners were manufacturers or workers in factories or stores. Other northerners were farmers.

The South is the states south of Washington, D.C. People from the South are called southerners. Most southerners were farmers. There were not many factories in the South.

1

In 1858, Minnesota became a state. It is part of the Midwest. In 1859, Oregon became a state. Oregon and California are part of the West. By 1859, the United States had 33 states and some territories.

Factories

Most factories were in the North. Many of them were in New England. Workers had to work very hard in the factories. They worked for 12 to 14 hours a day. They worked six days a week. Some men worked in factories. But many women and children worked in these factories, too.

In the 1830s and 1840s, some owners of some factories wanted to pay their workers less money for their work. These workers got angry. They did not want to get less money. They also wanted to work for only ten hours a day. In each factory, the workers talked about these things.

In factories, some workers wanted to change some things in their factory. They all had the same kind of job. So they had meetings. They talked about their job. They wanted the owner to listen to them. They decided that one worker could talk to the owner for all the workers. They said that together the workers could have more power. The workers would be called a union.

In the 1830s and 1840s, only a few factories had unions. Many workers were not members of unions. Some workers did not want the owner to get angry. They wanted to keep their jobs. So they did not join the union. Other workers thought that they were good workers. They thought that the owner would pay them more money for their hard work. They did not think that a union could help them.

People worked in factories.

Most owners did not want unions in their factories. They did not want any trouble with their workers. Most unions were not strong. The owners did not listen to the unions.

In 1837, Americans had trouble with money. They could not buy many things. So many factories had to close. Many Americans lost their jobs. They tried to find new jobs. They did not think about unions.

Before 1842, there were no laws about unions. Some workers started a union in a factory in Massachusetts. The owner did not want a union in his factory. The owner and the workers had a fight. Then the court in Massachusetts had to decide if the workers could have a union. In 1842, the court said that the workers had a right to have unions in Massachusetts. Then workers in other states wanted this right, too.

By 1844, there was a law about workers in the federal government. It said that these workers had to work for only ten hours a day. In 1844, Sarah Bagley started a union in a factory in Massachusetts. She asked the state government to make the same law for all of the workers in Massachusetts. But the state government did not make this law. Workers still had to work for more than ten hours a day.

In the 1840s, some unions were strong. Sometimes, the owners wanted the workers to work more hours. Other times, the owners wanted to pay less money to the workers. Some unions told workers that they should not work. The members of these unions went on strike. Then the owners had to find other workers or close their factories.

Owners of factories could always find other workers. They could give jobs to African Americans and immigrants. These people did not always have jobs. So they would work for less money than members of a union. The owners did not need the workers in a union. Most times, they did not listen to the unions.

By 1850, there were still not many unions. Many workers still worked hard for very little money. Often, young children worked all day in the factories. Sometimes, the factories were not safe places.

Transportation

By 1820, there were many factories in the North and big farms in the Midwest. Americans wanted better ways to carry things between the North and the Midwest. They wanted more roads and canals. Then these trips would cost less money. They would not take so much time. By 1850, companies, state governments, and the federal government had built some new roads and canals.

Before 1800, people did not know how to make machines with motors. An engine is a special kind of motor. After 1800, people learned how to make engines. So people made engines for railroads and ships. By 1850, many railroads traveled between the North and the Midwest. Many ships with engines carried things on the Mississippi River.

This ship had an engine.

Other ships with engines traveled on the ocean. They could take things from New Orleans to other American ports. They could also travel to Europe and Asia. American merchants could send things faster to other parts of the world. By the 1850s, American ships were the best in the world. The United States was getting rich.

Immigrants in the United States

Between 1830 and 1850, many more immigrants came to the United States. They came from Ireland, Germany, England, and other countries.

Some immigrants came to the United States because they wanted to own good land. Other immigrants did not like the governments in their old countries. Many immigrants thought that they could get rich in the United States.

Some immigrants bought land. They became farmers. But many immigrants did not have enough money. They could not buy land. So they worked in factories in big towns and cities. These immigrants could not leave these places. They did not make enough money.

Many Americans did not like the immigrants. They knew that immigrants would work for less money. They were afraid that the immigrants would take their jobs.

Many Americans thought that they had the best way of life. But the immigrants did not have the same way of life as Americans. They did not wear the same kind of clothes. They did not speak English. They wanted to live near each other. Then they could talk to people from their old countries.

Most Americans were Protestants. Many immigrants were not Protestants. They had different religions. In cities in the North, many Americans and immigrants had fights. They fought about jobs and religion.

CHAPTER 2

Life in the South

Owners made their slaves work hard.

In 1850, most southerners were farmers. Many of them grew cotton. They sold it to manufacturers in the North and in Europe. Manufacturers made cloth from the cotton. People bought cloth and made their own clothes.

Manufacturers also started to make clothes. Then more people could buy clothes in stores. So the manufacturers in the North needed more cotton. They wanted to make more cloth and clothes. So they paid farmers a lot of money for cotton.

Some rich farmers wanted to grow more cotton and make more money. They bought more land. Then they needed more workers. So they bought more African American slaves.

Not all farmers in the South owned slaves. Some farmers worked for a land owner. Other farmers had to pay rent to a land owner. Other farmers owned small farms. These farmers did not need slaves.

Some southerners owned very large farms. These farms were called plantations. Many African Americans were slaves on plantations. Some owners took good care of their slaves. Other owners made their slaves work many hours every day. Sometimes, they even hit their slaves.

Most African Americans did not want to be slaves. But the owners would not let them leave the plantations. Some slaves tried to run away from their owners. They tried to go to the North, Canada, and other places. In these places, the laws said that people could not own slaves.

The Constitution said that slaves could not run away from their owners. So the owners could send men to find the runaway slaves. These men brought the slaves back to their owners. Sometimes, the owners hit these slaves. Other times, owners sold these slaves to other owners. These slaves had to leave their families.

The southern states had made state laws about slavery. These laws said that slaves could not fight against their owners. They also said that slaves did not have any rights. The southern states made sure that the slaves obeyed the federal and state laws about slavery.

After 1830, the southern states also made laws

about free African Americans. Some of these laws said that free African Americans would not have many rights. Free African Americans had to pay taxes. But they could not vote. Free African Americans could not go to school. People could not teach them how to read. Free African Americans had to carry a paper. This paper said that they were not slaves anymore.

Sometimes, the slaves fought against their owners. Nat Turner was a slave in Virginia. Turner had learned how to read. He read books about slavery. These books said that slavery was wrong. In 1831, Turner told other African Americans that they should not be slaves. He helped slaves to fight against their owners. But the army helped the owners. Turner and the slaves lost the fight.

A white man fought against Nat Turner.

The government of Virginia took Turner to court. The law said that people could not tell slaves to fight against their owners. The court said that Turner had broken this law. So the government killed him for this crime.

African Americans did not always have the same religions as Americans. But some Americans wanted more African Americans to become Protestants or Catholics. By 1831, many African Americans were Protestants or Catholics. But some state laws said that African Americans could not go to the same church as white Americans. Free African Americans had to pray in their own churches. But a white person had to be at the church when they prayed.

By 1850, the state governments in the South still said that only white men could vote. Voters still had to be land owners. Owners of plantations had a lot of power. Some of them were representatives in the federal and state governments. Other owners of plantations talked to their representatives. These representatives made laws. These laws were good for the owners of slaves. These laws did not help slaves or free African Americans.

CHAPTER 3

People's Rights

Americans Start Groups

In the 1830s, Americans started new groups. These groups had meetings. At the meetings, they talked about different laws. Each group wanted laws about one special thing. The leaders of these groups could talk to their representatives. They could talk for all the members of the group.

One group decided that they did not want anyone to drink liquor. They wrote some little books. These books said that people should not drink liquor. This group talked to representatives in the government.

In 1834, Congress made a law about liquor. This law said that Americans could not sell liquor to first Americans. But Americans could buy liquor. Only a few people obeyed this law.

In 1846, the state government of Maine made a law about liquor. It said that people in Maine could not drink liquor.

In 1841, Dorothea Dix was upset about the jail near Boston. It was cold and dirty. Some people in the jail had broken the laws. Other people in the jail borrowed money and could not pay it back. Other people in the jail could not learn how to think well. Old people, young people, men, and women had to live together in the same parts of the jail.

Dorothea Dix

Dix wanted the government to make the jails better. So she talked to the representatives in the state government of Massachusetts. After a while, the representatives made new laws about jails. Then the jails in Massachusetts were better places.

Before 1848, women had very few rights. The laws said that women could not do many things. Women could not vote. Most women could not own land. They could not keep their own money. They had to give all of it to the men in their families. At meetings, women could not talk about the government.

In 1848, some women had a meeting about their rights. Elizabeth Cady Stanton and Lucretia Mott were the leaders at this meeting. They said that women should have more rights. Then the group talked to their representatives. But the representatives did not change the laws about women for many years.

Groups against Slavery

By the 1820s, many northern states had laws against slavery. People in these states could not own slaves. But there were no federal laws against slavery.

Some northerners and southerners thought that slavery was wrong. Some people thought that slavery was against their religion.

Some white Americans and free African Americans started groups. These groups wanted to help free African Americans and slaves. They did not want the free African Americans to become slaves again. They also thought that all slaves should be free after a while.

These groups knew that a government could make a law against slavery. England had made this kind of law in 1834. Members of these groups wrote little books. These books said that slavery was wrong. Members of these groups talked to their representatives. They asked Congress and more state governments to make laws against slavery. But these state governments did not make these laws.

Frederick Douglass

Frederick Douglass was a member of a group against slavery. He had been a slave. At meetings, Douglass told people about his life. He wanted to stop slavery right away.

13

William Lloyd Garrison

William Lloyd Garrison was a member of another group against slavery. Garrison was a white American. In his newspaper, he wrote that slavery was wrong.

Harriet Tubman

Harriet Tubman had been a slave. She ran away from her owner. In the North, she became a member of another group against slavery. This group was called the Underground Railroad. It helped slaves to run away from their owners.

Tubman went back to the South many times. She told slaves about safe homes on the way to the North. Slaves could stay in these homes. The owners

14

of these homes would not send slaves back to their owners. So the owners could not find their slaves. The Underground Railroad helped many slaves to go to the North. Then these slaves thought that they were safe and free.

Douglass, Garrison, Tubman, and other people worked against slavery. They wanted people to think that slavery was wrong. But many Americans in the North and in the South did not think this way.

Americans Think about Slavery

Many northerners and even some southerners thought that slavery was wrong. These people did not own slaves. Many southerners were afraid that slaves would fight against all white people. Southerners were also afraid that free African Americans would help the slaves in their fights. Many southerners did not want a federal law against slavery. They thought that it would start fights between white Americans and African Americans.

Many slave owners and other southerners said that owners took good care of their slaves. They said that the workers in the North did not live better than the slaves. They said that owners gave a lot of food to their slaves. But the workers in the North did not make a lot of money for their work. Sometimes, they could not buy enough food for their families.

Many northerners did not want to stop slavery. Some workers were afraid that free African Americans would take their jobs. These workers knew that African Americans could not always get jobs. So they would take less money for their work. The leaders of the unions would not let African Americans join their union.

Other northerners were manufacturers. They needed cotton from the South. They knew that the southerners needed slaves. Then they could grow a lot of cheap cotton. If southerners had to pay workers, cotton would cost more money. So these northerners did not want a law against slavery.

In 1798, two southern states did not want the people in their states to have to obey federal laws. Many northerners thought that people in all of the states should always obey the federal laws. In the 1850s, these northerners were afraid that federal laws against slavery would make the southern states angry. Then they might leave the United States.

CHAPTER 4

Slavery

In 1850, Congress made many new laws. One law said that California could be a free state. The people in the New Mexico and Utah territories would decide about slavery in their territories. If slaves ran away, the federal government would help owners to get their slaves back.

Many Americans thought that these laws would stop the fights between the states. They would not want to fight about slavery and land anymore.

By 1852, many Americans were not happy with these laws. Many northerners helped the runaway slaves. Many southerners got angry. They wanted the northerners to obey the law about runaway slaves. They also wanted more parts of the territories to become slave states.

In 1852, Americans had to vote for the next president. The Democrats wanted Franklin Pierce to be the next president. The Whigs wanted General Winfield Scott to be president. Americans voted. Pierce became the next president.

In the 1850s, some Americans wanted the United States to own more land. Cuba was a Spanish colony off the coast of Florida. Some people in Cuba owned slaves. The United States had tried to buy Cuba from Spain. But Spain would not sell Cuba.

Many southerners wanted Cuba to become a state. They wanted another slave state. But the United States would have to fight a war to get Cuba. Many northerners did not want another slave state. They also did not want to fight a war against Spain.

President Pierce said that the United States would not fight a war against Spain. Cuba would not become part of the United States.

In 1854, a lot of the Louisiana Territory was not states yet. Then Congress changed the Missouri Compromise law. The new law said that the people in the Louisiana Territory could decide about slavery in their land. A large part of the Louisiana Territory became two territories. They were called Kansas and Nebraska.

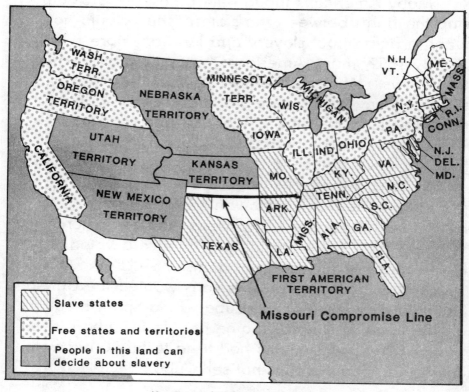

Kansas and Nebraska Territories

Northerners wanted Kansas to be a free state. Southerners wanted Kansas to become a slave state. So many southerners and northerners moved to Kansas. Then they could vote about slavery and many other things in Kansas. Missouri was a slave state near Kansas. Many people from Missouri also wanted Kansas to be a slave state. So they went to Kansas and voted. The people in Kansas voted for a new government. This government wanted Kansas to be a slave state.

But many people in Kansas did not want slavery in their territory. They voted for another government. This government wanted Kansas to be a free state. It told Congress that Kansas should become a free state.

By 1855, the territory of Kansas had two different governments. The people in Kansas fought about slavery. Many people died in these fights. Congress also had many fights about Kansas.

In 1856, Americans had to vote for the next president. Some Whigs and some Democrats thought that slavery was wrong. These people started a new party. It was called the Republican Party. The Republicans did not want slavery in any of the territories. They wanted John Fremont to be the next president.

The Democrats wanted James Buchanan to be the next president. They thought that people in the territories should decide about slavery in their land. Americans voted. James Buchanan became the next president.

In 1857, people in Kansas were still fighting about their government. Congress was also fighting about Kansas. In 1858, Congress said that Kansas could not be a free state. It had to be a territory. Kansas did not become a state until 1861.

Dred Scott

In 1857, the Supreme Court had to think about slavery. Dred Scott was a slave. His owner had taken him to live in a free state. Then the owner took Scott back to a slave state. Some people told Scott that he did not have to be a slave anymore. He had lived in a free state. These people helped Scott to take his owner to court.

The Supreme Court said that Scott was still a slave. Slaves were not free because they had lived in a free state. Only owners could say that slaves could be free. Slaves did not have any rights. Slaves could not take someone to court.

In 1857, the Supreme Court also said that Congress could not make laws against slavery. Congress would have to make a new amendment to the Constitution. This amendment would say that no people in the United States could be slaves. But Congress did not make this amendment until 1865.

In 1859, many northerners did not want slavery in the South. These people gave some money to John Brown. Brown and some men went to a fort in Virginia. They tried to take guns from the fort. They wanted to give these guns to slaves. Then these slaves could fight against their owners.

Robert E. Lee and the army caught Brown and his men. The federal government had a trial for Brown. The court decided that Brown had broken the law. So men from the government killed Brown for his crime.

In 1860, Americans had to vote for the next president. The Democrats in the South did not think that Congress should make a law against slavery in the territories. These Democrats wanted John Breckinridge to be the next president. The Democrats in the North thought that people in the territories should decide about slavery in their territory. These Democrats wanted Stephen Douglas to be the next president.

The Republicans wanted a law against slavery in the territories. They wanted Abraham Lincoln to be the next president. Americans had to think about the power of the state governments and the federal government. Americans voted. Abraham Lincoln became the next president.

Later in 1860, the government of South Carolina had a special meeting. At this meeting, the representatives talked about President Lincoln and Congress. They thought that Congress would make a law against slavery. So they decided that South Carolina did not want to be part of the United States anymore.

people in the United States could be slaves. But Congress did not make this amendment until 1865.

In 1859, many northerners did not want slavery in the South. These people gave some money to John Brown. Brown and some men went to a fort in Virginia. They tried to take guns from the fort. They wanted to give these guns to slaves. Then these slaves could fight against their owners.

Robert E. Lee and the army caught Brown and his men. The federal government had a trial for Brown. The court decided that Brown had broken the law. So men from the government killed Brown for his crime.

In 1860, Americans had to vote for the next president. The Democrats in the South did not think that Congress should make a law against slavery in the territories. These Democrats wanted John Breckinridge to be the next president. The Democrats in the North thought that people in the territories should decide about slavery in their territory. These Democrats wanted Stephen Douglas to be the next president.

The Republicans wanted a law against slavery in the territories. They wanted Abraham Lincoln to be the next president. Americans had to think about the power of the state governments and the federal government. Americans voted. Abraham Lincoln became the next president.

Later in 1860, the government of South Carolina had a special meeting. At this meeting, the representatives talked about President Lincoln and Congress. They thought that Congress would make a law against slavery. So they decided that South Carolina did not want to be part of the United States anymore.

CHAPTER 5

The Civil War

The army of the Confederacy took over Fort Sumter.

The War Starts

Early in 1861, many southerners thought that the Confederacy should own all the forts in the South. So the army of the Confederacy took over many of these forts. They also took over other federal buildings in the South. Then the United States had soldiers in only two forts in the South. One of these forts was Fort Sumter in South Carolina.

In March 1861, Lincoln became the president. He did not think that the southern states had the right to leave the United States. He thought that the United States still owned the forts and federal buildings in the South.

The leader of the army at Fort Sumter said that the fort needed many things. President Lincoln wanted the United States to keep this fort. He did not want the American army to fight against the army of the Confederacy. But he sent some things to Fort Sumter. He told the navy to bring them there. On April 12, the army of the Confederacy fought against the United States navy.

On April 13, the army of the Confederacy took over Fort Sumter. This fight started the War between the States. This war was also called the Civil War.

On April 17, Virginia decided to be part of the Confederacy, too. But many people in Virginia did not want to be part of the Confederacy. Most of these people lived in the western part of the state. They made their own government. This government wanted to be part of the United States. But West Virginia did not become a state until 1863. By May 20, Arkansas, Tennessee, and North Carolina also decided to be part of the Confederacy.

Delaware, Maryland, Kentucky, and Missouri were slave states. They were between the Confederacy and the other states. They were called the border states.

President Lincoln knew that the United States needed the border states. Washington, D.C., was between Maryland and Virginia. President Lincoln wanted northerners to be able to get to Washington, D.C. He did not want them to have to go through a state in the Confederacy.

People in Maryland fought about the Confederacy

and the United States. President Lincoln sent the army to Maryland. The army made sure that Maryland did not become part of the Confederacy. They also made sure that the people in Maryland did not help the Confederacy.

Most people in Delaware wanted to be part of the United States. The people in Missouri and Kentucky had many fights about the Confederacy.

The border states did not become part of the Confederacy. But most people from these states did not become soldiers in the United States army.

Americans did not all think the same way about the war. Some Americans wanted all the states to be part of the United States. They did not think that the southern states had the right to leave the United States. Other Americans thought that the states had the right to leave the United States.

Americans also thought different ways about slavery. Some Americans thought that people in the South should have the right to own slaves. Other Americans thought that there could be slavery in all parts of the United States. Other Americans did not want any slavery in the United States. But they did not want the southern states to leave the United States.

Some southerners fought in the army of the United States. Some northerners fought in the army of the Confederacy. Sometimes, men from the same families fought in different armies.

The North

In 1861, there were still 24 states in the United States. In this war, the states in the North and in the Midwest were called the North.

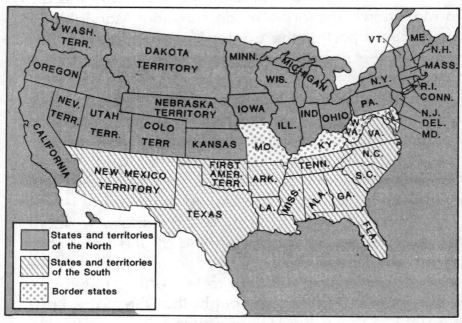

The United States in 1861

The North was richer than the South. It had many factories, roads, railroads, and banks. The factories made shoes, guns, clothes, and other things. Farmers grew a lot of food. Soldiers and other people in the North had enough food and clothes.

Merchants in the North traded with Europeans. Then they paid the taxes on imports to the federal government. The United States used this money for the war. But the United States needed more money for the war. So Congress made some new laws about taxes.

People get money for their work. This money is called income. One law said that a few people had to pay taxes on their incomes. Another law said that merchants had to pay more taxes on imports.

President Lincoln thought that the United States would win the war. He decided that the United States should do three things. The navy would make sure that ships stayed in the ports in the Confederacy. Then the Confederacy could not trade with other countries. The army would keep the soldiers in Texas, Arkansas, and Louisiana away from the soldiers in the rest of the Confederacy. The army also would take over Richmond, Virginia. The government of the Confederacy was in Richmond.

At first, some men said that they would be in the United States army. They were white Americans and free black Americans. After a while, President Lincoln needed more soldiers. In 1863, Congress made a new law. It said that all men between 20 and 45 years old had to join the army or navy. But the law also said that they could pay money to the government. Then they did not have to be soldiers. They could pay other people to be soldiers for them.

The South

In 1861, there were 11 states in the Confederacy. Many southerners thought that cotton would help the Confederacy during the war. The people in the South could trade with France and England. Then they could get things for the war.

The people in the South could not get enough food. The farmers in the South did not grow enough food. The people could not get food from the North anymore. There were not very many good roads in the South. So farmers could not bring much food to the cities.

There were only a few factories in the South. So people and soldiers in the South could not get cloth, shoes, guns, and other things. These things had to come from manufacturers in the North and in Europe.

During the war, southerners had a lot of trouble with money. The Confederacy made its own paper money. But sometimes, southerners had to pay a lot of this money for things. It was also hard to get many things. So things cost more and more money.

The Confederacy made its own paper money.

Jefferson Davis thought that the Confederacy could win the war. He knew that the Condederacy would fight this war on its own land. The soldiers in the Confederacy knew this land. Davis hoped that the northerners would get tired of the war. Then they would not fight anymore.

The army of the Confederacy decided to do two things. They wanted to take over Washington, D.C. Then the federal government could not do its work. They also wanted to keep the soldiers in the North away from the soldiers in the Midwest. Then the United States army could not fight very well.

At first, some men joined the army of the Confederacy. But Davis needed more soldiers in the army. So the government of the Confederacy made a law. It said that all white men between 18 and 35 years old had to be soldiers. But rich men could pay other men to be soldiers for them.

Many southerners did not want one strong government. They thought that each state should have a lot of power. Many state governments thought that they did not have to obey the laws of the Confederacy. So they did not send many soldiers to the army of the Confederacy.

At first, the Confederacy would not let slaves be in the army. Later, the Confederacy needed more soldiers. So the government said that slaves could be in the army. After the war, they would be free.

President Lincoln

Before the war, the members of Congress had been fighting about many kinds of laws. Some representatives from the North had wanted to make some laws. But the representatives from the South had voted against them. So Congress could not make some kinds of laws.

During the war, Congress and President Lincoln had to make laws for the United States. The southern states did not have representatives in Congress anymore. These representatives could not vote against federal laws. So the representatives from the northern states could make some new federal laws.

President Lincoln and Congress had to think about the land in the Midwest and the West. They wanted more farmers to live there. In 1862, Congress made a new law about this land. It said that people could make a farm on part of this land. They had to live on their land for five years. Then they could buy their land for very little money.

In 1862, President Lincoln and Congress also wanted more railroads. They gave money and land to some companies. These companies would build railroads from the Midwest to California. Then Americans could travel by railroad from the east coast to the west coast.

The Fights in the Civil War

In 1861, both the North and the South thought that countries in Europe would help them with the war. In 1861 and 1862, England and France helped the Confederacy. They wanted the Confederacy to become a new country. They knew that the Confederacy would not make laws about taxes on imports.

The Confederacy and the United States fought in the South. They also fought on the ocean near the

Soldiers from the North fought against soldiers from the South.

southern states. The armies fought in Virginia, Pennsylvania, Tennessee, Louisiana, Maryland, Arkansas, and Mississippi. Soldiers in the United States army had to learn about the land in the South. But the United States army had more soldiers and guns.

In 1861 and 1862, the United States army also fought against the first Americans west of the Mississippi River. So the United States army did not have many soldiers in the South. The army of the Confederacy won many fights against the United States army. But the United States would not stop this war.

In 1862, the United States army needed more soldiers to fight against the Confederacy. So it sent the soldiers in the Midwest to the South. Then the United States army started to win some fights.

The United States navy tried to keep ships in the South in their ports. Then they could not trade with European countries. The United States had many strong ships. Most of the time, the United States navy won the fights against the ships of the Confederacy. So these ships could not go to Europe.

The United States army tried to get more soldiers into the South by ship. They wanted to take over the cities in the South. But there were forts near the coast. Many soldiers of the Confederacy stayed in these forts. They did not want more soldiers from the United States army in the Confederacy. Many times, the army of the Confederacy won the fights near the forts. Then more soldiers in the United States army could not go into the South. They could not help the other soldiers to fight against the soldiers of the Confederacy.

By 1863, the United States and the Confederacy had been fighting the Civil War for almost two years. They were fighting about the right of states to leave the United States. They were not fighting about slavery yet.

Many northerners thought that slavery was wrong. They talked to President Lincoln. He thought that slavery was wrong, too. But he did not want the border states to become part of the Confederacy. So he did not say that the slaves in the border states should be free.

President Lincoln talked to men in the government about slavery.

In 1863, President Lincoln did say that some slaves should be free. These slaves lived in the states of the Confederacy. The United States army would help to make them free. Congress did not make a law against slavery. But the United States and the Confederacy started to fight about slavery.

By 1863, the United States started to win more fights. Then the European countries were afraid that the Confederacy would not win the war. They did not help the Confederacy anymore. The United States army won more fights.

Congress at the End of the War

In 1864, President Lincoln and Congress thought that the United States would win the war. They had to think about the states in the Confederacy. President Lincoln wanted them to be part of the United States again.

In 1864, Congress tried to make a new law. It told how the states in the Confederacy could become part of the United States again. The people in these states would have to do many things. Each southern state had to start a new state government. It also had to write a new state constitution. It had to say that all black Americans could be free. More than half of the voters had to say that they would obey the laws of the United States. Men from the government of the Confederacy could not be part of the new state governments. These men also could not vote.

President Lincoln thought that slavery was wrong. But he did not think that Congress had the right to make a law against slavery. He thought that this kind of law would be against the Constitution. So he vetoed this federal law. Congress could not make this law.

President Lincoln thought that the Constitution needed an amendment against slavery. All the states would have to decide if this amendment could become part of the Constitution. Later in 1864, Congress wrote the 13th Amendment. It said that there should be no slavery in the United States or in its territories. Then the states had to vote about this amendment.

In 1864, Americans had to vote for the next president. Only men in the United States could vote. Men in the Confederacy could not vote. The United States and the Confederacy were still fighting the war.

The Republicans wanted President Lincoln to be president for four more years. They wanted all the states to be part of the United States. They also wanted the slaves to be free. The Democrats wanted General George McClellan to be the next president. They did not think that the United States should fight this war anymore. Americans voted. President Lincoln became the president again.

The End of the War

For four years, the United States fought against the Confederacy. Many soldiers and other people died in these fights. Soldiers burned down many houses and farms in the South.

On April 2, 1865, the armies were fighting against each other in Richmond, Virginia. General Robert E. Lee was the leader of the army of the Confederacy. General Ulysses S. Grant was the leader of the United States army. General Lee and the army of the Confederacy left Richmond. General Grant and the United States army went after them. The United States army won this fight.

On April 9, Lee and Grant met in Appomattox, Virginia. Grant gave a special paper to Lee. It said that the war was over. Grant and Lee wrote their names on this paper. Then the war was over.

CHAPTER 6

The United States after the War

President Lincoln

President Lincoln wanted to help the southern states. He wanted them to be part of the United States again. So he sent soldiers to these states. They would help the southerners to start new state governments.

Many members of Congress did not want to help the southern states. They wanted Congress to make some new kinds of laws. But they knew that the representatives from the South would vote against these laws. So they did not want the representatives from the South to be in Congress. President Lincoln and Congress had many fights about the southern states.

President Lincoln talked to men at the House of Representatives.

After the war, many white Americans in the South did not have homes. During the war, soldiers had burned down their houses and farms. They could not grow food anymore. Some of them got sick and died.

After the war, enough states said that the 13th Amendment should become part of the Constitution. So the Constitution said that black Americans were not slaves anymore. They had to take care of themselves. Some land owners gave some black Americans a little land. Other land owners let them pay rent for land. But many black Americans did not have a place to live. They did not have food. They did not know how to read and write. Some black Americans could get jobs. But most did not have jobs. Some of them moved to the North. Some black Americans got sick and died.

Black Americans learned many things at the Freedmen's Bureau.

In 1865, President Lincoln and Congress started the Freedmen's Bureau. It would help black Americans and poor, white Americans in the South. It would help them to start a new life. It would give them food, clothes, and land.

Many northerners and southerners thought that the Freedmen's Bureau would help people in the South. But many southerners did not like the Freedmen's Bureau. They thought that it would help black Americans to fight against white Americans.

President Lincoln and Congress talked about the southern states. They said that the southern states would have to obey the Constitution and federal laws. The 13th Amendment was part of the Constitution. But Congress and President Lincoln could not decide how the southern states could become part of the United States again.

On April 14, 1865, John Wilkes Booth shot President Lincoln. The next day, the president died. Andrew Johnson was the vice president. He became the next president.

President Andrew Johnson

At first, President Johnson did not want to help the southern states to be part of the United States again. He wanted Jefferson Davis and other leaders of the Confederacy to go to jail. Men in the federal government found some of these people and put them in jail.

Later, President Johnson decided that the southern states should not have so much trouble. But many members of Congress did not think the same way.

By December 1865, most southern states had new constitutions. They had also started new state governments. President Johnson said that these states could be part of the United States again. So they sent new representatives to Congress. Most of these representatives had been leaders in the Confederacy. Congress said that these representatives from the South could not be part of Congress. So the South still did not have any representatives in Congress.

Some members of Congress did not like the new constitutions in some southern states. Some constitutions said that black Americans could not have many rights. So in 1866, Congress made laws about the rights of black Americans. The southern states would have to obey these laws. One law said that black Americans should have the same rights as white Americans. Another law gave more powers to the Freedmen's Bureau.

President Johnson vetoed these laws. He said that Congress could not make laws without the representatives from the South. He also said that the federal government could not make laws about some of these rights. Only state governments could make those kinds of laws.

Many members of Congress wanted these laws. So Congress voted again. Enough members of Congress did not want President Johnson to veto these laws. So Congress voted for these laws again. President Johnson could not veto these laws again. So Americans had to obey these laws.

In 1866, some members of Congress liked these laws about black Americans. But they were afraid that the Supreme Court would have to decide about these laws. It might say that these laws were against the Constitution. So Congress wrote another new amendment to the Constitution.

The 14th Amendment says that no state can take away the rights of any American. States may not make laws against the rights of black Americans. This amendment does not say that the states have to let black Americans vote. But it did say that all black Americans have to have representatives in Congress. The 14th Amendment also said that leaders of the Confederacy could not be part of the state or federal government.

In 1866, all state governments had to vote about the 14th Amendment. The southern states had to vote for this amendment. Then they could become part of the United States again.

In 1866, Tennessee said that the 14th Amendment should be part of the Constitution. Then Congress said that Tennessee could send representatives to Congress again. All of the other southern states voted against the 14th Amendment. So they could not send representatives to Congress.

In 1867, ten southern states still did not have representatives in Congress. Congress made a new law about these states. It said many things. The new constitutions of the southern states had to say that black Americans could vote. Black men also had the right to be part of the government. The leaders of the Confederacy could not vote or be part of the government. The states also had to vote for the 14th Amendment. Then Congress would let these states send representatives to Congress. These states would become part of the United States again. The army would make sure that the southern states obeyed this law.

The people in the southern states made new governments and wrote new constitutions. By 1868, many southern states said that they would obey the federal laws and the Constitution. Then the 14th Amendment became part of the Constitution. North Carolina, South Carolina, Florida, Arkansas, Louisiana, and Alabama joined the United States again. These states sent representatives to Congress.

By 1867, Congress and President Johnson had had many fights. Congress made some laws. But President Johnson vetoed many of these laws. Many members of Congress got angry.

In 1867, Congress made a new law about the power of the president. It said that the president could not just take jobs away from people in the government. The Senate also had to say that these people could not keep their jobs. President Johnson thought that this law was against the Constitution. He vetoed the law. But Congress voted again. It became a law, anyway.

The Senate had a trial for President Johnson.

In 1868, President Johnson said that the secretary of war could not keep his job anymore. Then many members of Congress said that President Johnson had broken this new law. They did not think that he should be president anymore. Then the Senate had a trial for the president. Many senators thought that President Johnson had broken the law. All the senators voted. The Senate said that President Johnson could keep his job.

Later in 1868, Americans had to vote for the next president. The Republicans did not want President Johnson to be president for four more years. They wanted General Ulysses Grant to be the next president. The Democrats wanted Horatio Seymour to be the next president. Americans voted. Grant became the next president.

CHAPTER 7

The South after the Civil War

The State Governments

After the Civil War, many northerners moved to the South. Some northerners wanted to make sure that black Americans got all their rights. They became part of the state governments in the South. Other northerners wanted to make a lot of money. So they bought land in the South and started their own farms or companies. A few northerners stole money from the Freedmen's Bureau and from black Americans.

Some southerners never liked slavery. They had always wanted their states to be part of the United States. They had not fought in the army of the Confederacy. After the war, they wanted to become part of the new state governments and the federal government. They wanted black Americans to have all of their rights.

In 1867, Congress had made laws about voters. One law said that black Americans could vote. Another law said that people from the government of the Confederacy could not vote. These laws helped some white Americans and some black Americans to become part of the federal and new state governments.

By 1868, seven southern states had become part of the United States again. Many northerners and southerners became part of these governments. They helped to make new laws. These laws gave rights to black Americans.

Before 1868, state governments in the South did not spend a lot of money. But the new state governments decided to build new roads, schools, and other things. They spent a lot of money for these things. The new state governments made some new laws. Some laws gave more rights to women. Other new laws gave more rights to poor people.

Many southerners did not like these new state governments. They did not think that northerners or black Americans should be part of their governments. They thought that the leaders of the Confederacy should be able to vote. These people started new groups.

One of these groups was called the Ku Klux Klan. Members of these groups fought against black Americans and some white Americans. They did not want these people to be part of the government. They did not want them to vote. Sometimes, members of these groups burned down houses and killed people.

These people in the South were members of the Ku Klux Klan.

43

Laws about Voters

In 1869, Congress wanted to make sure that the southern states would let black Americans vote. So Congress wrote a new amendment to the Constitution. The 15th Amendment says that black Americans have the right to vote.

In 1870, the 15th Amendment became part of the Constitution. Then all the state governments had to let black Americans vote.

Mississippi, Virginia, Georgia, and Texas were not part of the United States. They could not send representatives to Congress yet. These states had to say that they would obey the 15th Amendment and the rest of the Constitution. Then Congress would let them be part of the United States again. In 1870, these states became part of the United States.

Sometimes, some southerners wanted to pick their representatives. They were afraid that the voters would not vote for these people. So they did not count all the votes.

In 1870, Congress made some laws. These laws said that the president could send men to the South. These men would help to count votes in the South. The president could also send the army to stop fights in the South. President Grant sent men and soldiers to the South. These men counted the votes. The soldiers helped to make sure that black Americans could vote.

In 1872, Congress made a new law. It said that men from the government of the Confederacy could vote. But these men did not want black Americans to vote. They also did not want black Americans to be part of the government. But the army helped black Americans to keep their rights.

White Americans helped black Americans to vote in the South.

Black Americans

In 1877, the army left the southern states. Then the southern states tried to make sure that black Americans could not vote. They made new laws about voters. Some of these laws said that all voters had to pay a special tax. Many black Americans were very poor. They could not pay this money. So they could not vote. Other laws said that voters had to know how to read and write. People had not taught black Americans how to read and write. So many of these people could not vote.

Congress had made a law about the rights of black Americans. It said that black Americans and white Americans could use the same places. They could use the same trains and eat in the same restaurants. But this law did not say anything about schools.

In 1883, the Supreme Court said that this law was against the Constitution. The 14th Amendment said that states could not take rights away from black Americans. But it did not say anything about companies. So companies could say that black Americans could not ride on their trains or eat in their restaurants.

By 1890, all southern states had new laws about black Americans. These laws were called Jim Crow laws. They said many things. White Americans and black Americans had to ride in different railroad cars. Black Americans and white Americans had to go to different parts of a park. There were some schools for black Americans and other schools for white Americans.

In 1896, the Supreme Court said that these state laws were not against the 14th Amendment. The southern state governments could make these kinds of laws.

CHAPTER 8

The Presidents: 1869-1896

President Grant

President Ulysses S. Grant

The president and representatives can give jobs to other people. They can also take these jobs away. Sometimes, they do not think about these workers. They just want to give jobs to people in their party. So they take jobs away from some people. Then they give them to people in their party.

In 1869, President Grant said that some more Republicans would have jobs in the federal government. Some Democrats lost their jobs. Many Republicans in Congress also gave jobs to many people in their party. Then they thought that the Republicans would be stronger.

In 1871, Congress made a law about some jobs in the federal government. This law started a new group in the government. Only this group could pick people for some jobs in the federal government.

Representatives could not pick people for these jobs. These jobs are called civil service jobs. But Congress did not let this group do its work. By 1875, this group stopped its work.

In 1872, Americans had to vote for the next president. Some Republicans wanted President Grant to be president for four more years. Other Republicans and the Democrats wanted Horace Greeley to be the next president. Americans voted. President Grant was the president for the next four years.

In 1872, Congress talked about money for the railroad companies. The federal government had told these companies to build a railroad across the United States. The government would pay the companies for this work. The companies built the railroad. They said that it cost a lot of money. The federal government had not said that they would pay the companies so much money.

Congress had to vote about this money. Some members of Congress did not think that the railroad should cost so much money. So the companies gave money to some members of Congress. Then these members voted to give all the money to the railroad companies. The federal government paid all the money to the companies.

Many people thought that President Grant was honest. He said that some people could work in the government. He thought that these people would be good workers. But some of these people were not honest. Some of them stole money from the government. Sometimes, companies gave money to these people. Then they let the companies break some laws.

Many Americans wanted more honest workers in the government. They did not want representatives to pick people for so many jobs. These Americans wanted the special group for civil service jobs again. They wanted this group to do its work. It should make sure that more honest people worked in the government.

President Hayes

President Rutherford Hayes

In 1876, Americans had to vote for the next president. The Democrats wanted Samuel Tilden to be the next president. The Republicans wanted Rutherford Hayes to be the next president. Both men said that they wanted more honest men in the federal government.

More Americans voted for Tilden than for Hayes. But more electors voted for Hayes. The Constitution says that Americans vote for electors. Then the electors vote for president. In four states, there were fights about the votes of the electors. Congress told a special group to count the votes of the electors in these states. This special group said that Hayes won in these four states. Hayes became the next president.

In 1877, some railroad companies decided to pay less money to their workers. So some of these workers went on strike. The state armies fought against the workers. But the workers would not go back to work. Then President Hayes sent some federal soldiers. These soldiers also fought against the workers. Many people were hurt in these fights. Some soldiers worked the trains. Then people could still use the railroads.

At last, the strike was over. Many workers went back to their jobs. Some of them became members of unions. They wanted federal laws to help the unions.

Presidents Garfield and Arthur

In 1880, Americans had to vote for the next president. President Hayes decided that he did not want to be president anymore. The Republicans wanted James Garfield to be the next president. The Democrats wanted General Winfield Hancock to be the next president. Americans voted. Garfield became the next president.

In 1881, someone shot President Garfield. Americans did not have to vote again. Chester Arthur was the vice president. He became the next president.

President James A. Garfield

President Chester A. Arthur

In 1883, no jobs in the federal government were civil service jobs. So President Arthur and Congress made a new law about some jobs in the federal government. These jobs would become civil service jobs. Representatives could not pick people for these jobs. This law started a new special group. It would make tests for these jobs. People must take the tests. Then some of them could get civil service jobs. The law said that the president also could make other jobs become civil service jobs. Then workers would have to take a test for these jobs, too.

President Cleveland

**President
Grover Cleveland**

In 1884, some Republicans did not want President Arthur to be the president for four more years. They wanted James Blaine to be the next president. Blaine did not think that there should be civil service jobs.

Other Republicans wanted these jobs to be civil service jobs. These Republicans and the Democrats wanted Grover Cleveland to be the next president. Cleveland thought that these tests would help the government. They would help the government to pick honest workers. Americans voted. Cleveland became the next president.

In 1884, representatives could still pick people for many jobs. So President Cleveland and Congress decided that more jobs should become civil service jobs.

President Cleveland and Congress had to think about big companies. They decided that railroads and other companies had taken land from the federal government. In 1887, the federal government made these companies give the land back.

The railroad companies and other big companies were not always honest. Sometimes, they had different prices for different people. They had offices in many states. In 1887, Congress made a law about this kind of company. This law started a special group.

This group is called the Interstate Commerce Commission (ICC). It makes rules for railroad companies. Railroad companies have to obey these rules. The rules say that railroad companies have to have the same price for everybody. The ICC can take the railroad companies to court. Americans can talk to members of the ICC. Then the ICC talks to the railroad companies. The ICC can also make new rules.

President Harrison

In 1888, Americans had to vote for the next president. The Democrats wanted President Cleveland to be the president for four more years. President Cleveland had helped many farmers and owners of small companies. These people wanted him to be president again. The Republicans wanted Benjamin Harrison to be the next president. Harrison wanted Congress to put high taxes on imports. He wanted to help rich people and big companies.

Americans voted. More Americans voted for Cleveland than for Harrison. But more electors voted for Harrison than for Cleveland. So Harrison became the next president.

**President
Benjamin Harrison**

Many companies were getting bigger. Some companies sold the same things. Each company wanted to sell more of these things than other companies. Sometimes, these companies had fights about prices. One company would make their prices lower. Then another company would do the same thing. Soon the companies thought that they were not making enough money. So some companies got together. They decided that all the companies would have the same price for the same thing. Then they could make the price high. People had to pay that high price. They had to buy this thing from these companies.

People got angry. They did not want to pay high prices for things. They talked to members of Congress. In 1890, Congress made a law against big companies. This law was the first federal law about big companies. It said that companies could not decide on the same price for one thing. The federal government could make a big company become many small companies.

President Harrison thought that workers and farmers would like this law. But the government did not make companies obey the law. Many companies still got much bigger. They still made high prices.

In 1890, Congress also made a new law about taxes on imports. It said that merchants had to pay more taxes on some imports. Then Americans had to pay more money for these things. This law helped American manufacturers.

In the 1890s, some Americans thought that the federal government helped big companies and rich people too much. They started the Populist Party. They wanted the federal government to help workers and farmers. They wanted the government to own railroads and other companies. They thought that rich people should pay higher taxes on their incomes. But most people should pay low taxes on their incomes.

In 1892, Americans had to vote for the next president. The Republicans wanted President Harrison to be president for four more years. They thought that President Harrison would help big companies.

The Populists and some Democrats wanted James Weaver to be the next president. Most Democrats wanted Grover Cleveland to be the next president. He had been the president from 1884 to 1888. These Democrats thought that President Cleveland had helped workers and farmers. He wanted to make the taxes on imports lower. Americans voted. Cleveland became the president again.

President Cleveland

In 1893, Americans had trouble with money. Many people did not have enough money for food. Most Americans could not buy very many things. So some factories had to close. Some owners and bankers lost their money. Some workers lost their jobs. A few companies were still open. They could make very high prices. People were angry. But they needed some things. They had to buy things from these companies.

Farmers had to pay a lot of money to send food to the cities. So they made the price of food higher. Then they did not sell so much food. But they still needed money. Many banks would not let farmers borrow any more money. Many farmers lost their farms.

In 1894, Congress made a new law about taxes. It made taxes on imports lower. It also said that more Americans would have to pay taxes on their incomes. These Americans were not very rich. But they had to pay a small tax on their incomes.

In 1895, the Supreme Court decided that Congress could not make laws about taxes on income. Then Americans did not have to pay taxes on their incomes anymore.

In 1895, the Supreme Court also decided that the federal government could make laws about trade between states. But it could not make a law about trade inside a state. So many companies could still get bigger. A few companies got very big.

In 1896, Americans had to vote for the next president. Some Democrats did not want President Cleveland to be president for four more years. These Democrats decided that they wanted William Jennings Bryan to be the next president. The Populists also wanted Bryan to become the next president. The Republicans wanted William McKinley to be the next president. McKinley wanted to help the owners of big companies. Americans voted. McKinley became the next president.

CHAPTER 9

The West from 1864 to 1896

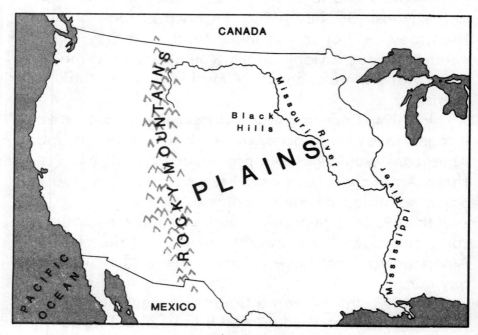

The Plains

The First Americans

Before 1849, the federal government had made many tribes move to the territories. Many Americans thought that first Americans did not know how to take care of themselves. In 1849, Congress started a new group. This group sent men to the land of the first Americans. They would help the tribes in their new land.

Many of these men were honest. But many times, the federal government did not give enough money to these men. So they could not help all the first Americans. Some of these men were not honest.

They stole from the first Americans and the federal government.

In 1850, many tribes lived on land in the territories. Some parts of the territories were flat and dry. This land was called the Plains. The land of the Plains was part of the Louisiana Territory. It is east of the Rocky Mountains.

Only a few Americans lived on the Plains. Many first Americans lived on the Plains. They hunted for animals. Some of these animals were buffaloes. The first Americans used the buffaloes for food. They also used the skins of buffaloes to make clothes and homes.

In 1862, Congress said that farmers and railroad companies could own some land in the territories. After 1862, many more Americans started to move to the Plains. They built farms. Companies built railroads. Some Americans brought sheep and cattle to this land. They built ranches. Other Americans on the Plains were miners. They looked for gold and silver.

In 1866, Congress started to make new kinds of laws about first Americans. These laws said that some tribes had to live on special land. It was called a reservation. These tribes of first Americans could not move to other land. Americans could not live on the land in the reservations.

By 1869, railroads went through the Plains. So more Americans came to live on the Plains. But the first Americans did not want more Americans to live on the Plains. Americans wanted the tribes on the Plains to live on reservations. They talked to members of Congress. Then Congress made treaties with some tribes on the Plains. These treaties said that these tribes had to move to reservations.

Most reservations were not big. Some of the reservations were far away from the old land of the tribe. First Americans had to stay on the reservations. They could not hunt for buffaloes anymore. So they could not use buffaloes for food. They had to grow all their food. Many first Americans got sick and died on the reservations.

Sometimes, first Americans tried to leave their reservations. The American army built forts near them. It tried to make the tribes stay on their reservations. The army killed many, many buffaloes. Then there were not many buffaloes on the Plains anymore. The first Americans did not leave the reservations to hunt for them.

The American army killed many buffaloes.

The United States had made a treaty with a tribe on the Plains. This tribe was the Sioux. The United States told the Sioux to live on a reservation in the Black Hills. The Black Hills are on the Plains.

In 1874, Americans found gold in the Black Hills. Many Americans went to the Black Hills to find gold. They did not want the Sioux to stay on this land. The Sioux did not want Americans on their reservation. They thought that the Black Hills were very special.

In 1875, the army told the Sioux to move to a new reservation. This reservation was not in the Black Hills. The Sioux did not want to move. The army and the Sioux fought about this land for two years.

In the 1880s, some Americans thought that the United States should give more rights to the first Americans. The United States should not make them live on reservations. But other Americans wanted the first Americans to live on the reservations.

Some Americans wanted first Americans to own the land on their reservations. They wanted to help the first Americans. But the federal laws said that first Americans could not own this land. The United States owned this land. The first Americans could not sell it.

Other Americans were not honest. They wanted the first Americans to own the land on their reservations. Then they could buy this land from the first Americans. They could sell it for a lot more money and get rich.

In 1887, Congress made a law about the land of first Americans. It said that some first Americans could own land on their reservations. Many members of Congress thought that this law would help many first Americans. They would become more like other Americans.

Some members of Congress did not think that first Americans could take care of their land. So the law also said that first Americans could not sell their land for 25 years.

After 1887, first Americans could own land on the reservations. Other Americans could also own land there. Most of the time, first Americans got the bad land. Americans got most of the good land.

New States

Between 1864 and 1896, many more Americans moved to the territories. Many Americans bought land on the reservations and other land. They built farms and ranches. They dug mines. They also built towns and started governments.

After a while, many Americans lived in one part of a territory. Then they asked Congress if their land could become a state. Congress talked about each new state. Then the members of Congress voted.

In 1864, Congress said that Nevada could become a state. In 1867, Nebraska became a state. In 1876, Colorado became a state. In 1889, North Dakota, South Dakota, Montana, and Washington became states. In 1890, Idaho and Wyoming became states. In 1896, Utah became a state. By 1896, there were 45 states in the United States. The United States still owned some territories.

CHAPTER 10

The United States Changes

New Machines

Before 1865, people did not know how to make telephones, electricity, or cars. Between 1865 and 1896, Americans and Europeans learned how to make these things. They also learned how to make new kinds of machines. Some new machines helped workers to make things in factories. New kinds of factories opened in cities.

Before 1850, people used oil from animals. They burned this oil in lamps to make light. After 1850, people found oil in the ground. Americans started to dig for this kind of oil. People could use this oil to make light in their lamps. People also found coal in the ground. They used oil and coal to keep their homes warm.

By 1882, some people knew about electricity. Then people could build special factories to make electricity. These factories used water, oil, or coal. Some cities built factories for electricity. People in these cities could use electricity to make light. Electricity also made machines work better.

By the 1880s, people could build better railroads. These railroads could travel faster. There were railroads in many parts of the United States.

In 1837, Samuel Morse made a new kind of machine. This machine is called a telegraph. People could use a telegraph to send a special kind of letter.

It is called a telegram. In one day, people could send telegrams from one place to another. Sometimes, it took many weeks to send a letter. People from the railroad companies used the telegraph. By 1896, there were telegraphs in many towns and cities.

Samuel Morse made the first telegraph.

In 1876, Alexander Bell made another machine. This machine is called a telephone. People could talk to other people on the telephone. Before 1896, there were not many telephones. Most people did not have telephones in their homes.

Farmers

After the Civil War, more people worked in factories. They lived in cities. So farmers sold more food to people in the cities. It was hard work to grow a lot of food. Most farmers did not have electricity or many machines.

In the 1870s, farmers wanted to make a lot of money. So they grew a lot of food. But Americans did not need so much food. Then farmers wanted to sell food to Europeans. But farmers in other countries also sold food to the Europeans. So American farmers could not sell much food in Europe.

Farmers had a lot of trouble with money. They had to send their things by railroad to the cities. They had to pay a lot of money to the railroad companies.

Farmers also had trouble with banks. Sometimes, they could not borrow money from the banks. Other times, they could borrow money from the banks. But the banks made them pay back the money and a lot of extra money.

Some farmers sold food to merchants. Then the merchants sold the food to people in the cities. The merchants did not pay a lot of money to the farmers. But the merchants sold the food for a lot of money. Farmers were angry at these merchants.

In the 1870s, farmers started groups. Together, their groups were called the Grange. The members of one group got together and sold all the food from their farms. Then they got more money for their food. They also bought things together. Then they did not have to pay so much money for things. But most of the time, members of the groups did not work well together.

In the 1870s, some members of the Grange talked to representatives. Then some state governments made laws about railroads. These laws said that the railroad companies had to have the same price for everybody. They could not make farmers pay more money for the same trip.

Farmers went to a meeting of the Grange.

In 1877, the Supreme Court said that the states could make laws about railroads in their state. But most railroads traveled between states. In 1886, the Supreme Court said that the state governments could not make laws about trade between the states. Then the state governments could not make laws about most railroads anymore.

Farmers still had to use the railroads. Members of the Grange talked to representatives in Congress. In 1887, Congress made a law about trade between the states. Railroad companies had to obey this law. Then farmers did not have so much trouble with railroads.

Unions

Between 1865 and 1896, more workers wanted to change things about their jobs. So some of them became members of unions. Workers with one kind of job joined one union in their factory. Workers with other kinds of jobs joined unions for their kind of job.

In 1866, different unions tried to make one big union for different kinds of workers. It was called the Knights of Labor. The leaders of this big union thought that together the small unions could be stronger. Then members of this big union talked to members of Congress. They wanted a federal law to help all workers.

Workers talked to the leaders of the Knights of Labor.

In 1868, Congress made a law about workers in the federal government. This law said that these workers had to work for only eight hours a day. But Congress did not make a law about all workers. Other workers still had to work for more than eight hours a day.

In the 1870s, some unions were stronger. They told more workers to go on strike. Sometimes, owners of factories listened to the union. Other times, they did not. There were big fights between unions and owners.

In 1886, many unions made another big union for many kinds of workers. This union was called the American Federation of Labor (AFL). Many unions from all parts of the United States became part of the AFL. Workers in these unions became members of the AFL. The AFL helped to make their unions stronger.

The AFL wanted many things for the unions. It did not want workers to work for more than eight hours a day and six days a week. It wanted owners to make their factories safer. It wanted workers to get more money for their work. It wanted all the workers in each factory to be members of the union. It did not want owners of these factories to give jobs to other workers.

The AFL helped many unions with their strikes. There were big, long strikes against the railroad companies and other companies. But the federal and state governments tried to stop the strikes in many ways. The army tried to stop a strike. The courts said that unions could not go on strike. Sometimes, the courts put the leader of a union into jail.

By 1896, only one worker out of ten was a member of a union. Many workers did not want to obey the rules of the union. They did not want to have to join the union.

Many unions did not let all workers become members of their union. Many black workers and women could not be members of some unions.

Immigrants in the United States

Between 1865 and 1896, many more immigrants came to the United States. They came from Russia, China, and many European countries.

Immigrants came to New York City.

Some American companies wanted workers to work for less money. So they brought many immigrants to the United States and gave them jobs. They did not pay these workers very much money for their work.

American workers did not like these immigrants. They were afraid that the immigrants would take their jobs. Some unions said that immigrants could not join their unions. Sometimes, immigrants would get jobs when a union went on strike.

Many workers wanted Congress to make laws against immigrants. They did not want so many immigrants to come to the United States. Congress did not make many of these laws. But in 1882, Congress made a law about immigrants from China. It said that these immigrants could not come to live in the United States.

Women

Between 1865 and 1896, many women worked in factories and other places. Women wanted some rights. They wanted to keep some of their own money. They wanted to be able to vote.

Groups of women talked to their representatives. Some state governments changed some laws about the rights of women. Some groups of women also asked the federal government to make laws about rights of women.

By 1900, some states had given more rights to women. Women in four western states could vote. But in the other states, women still could not vote. Congress did not make an amendment to the Constitution about women. Women had to fight for the right to vote for many more years.

CHAPTER 11

The United States and the World

Looking for New Land

Some things come from the land. People can not make these things. These things are called raw materials. Some raw materials are iron, silver, gold, oil, sugar cane, and cotton. In factories, workers make things out of raw materials.

In the 1800s, some countries did not have enough raw materials. Manufacturers knew that some land had a lot of raw materials. They wanted their governments to own this land. Then they could get more raw materials from this land.

Some strong countries sent their armies to take over these lands. They did not think that the people in these places had any rights. Sometimes, these people fought against the soldiers. But these people did not have strong governments and guns. They could not fight very well against the soldiers.

Most of the time, the armies won. Then their countries said that they owned the land. The land became a colony.

In the 1800s, England owned many colonies. Spain owned a few colonies. Other countries in Europe and Asia also owned a few colonies. These colonies were in Africa, parts of Asia, and other places.

The United States had a lot of raw materials. Americans did not need more land. But they knew that England was rich. It owned a lot of colonies.

Some Americans thought that the United States should own colonies. Then it would be richer.

In 1867, the United States bought some land from Russia. This land was north of Canada. It is called Alaska. Many Americans did not want the United States to own land so far away. Other Americans thought that Alaska would be good for the United States.

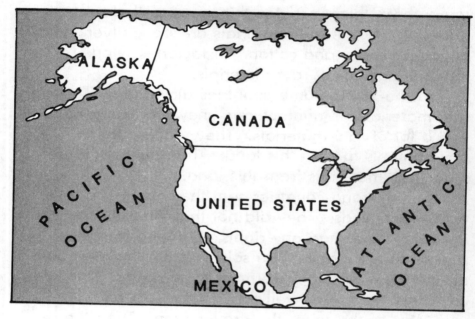

Alaska

In 1897, some people found gold in Alaska and sold it. They became rich. Then more Americans wanted the United States to own more land.

The Spanish-American War

In the 1890s, American merchants wanted to sell more things to people in other places. They did not want the United States to own colonies. But they did not want other countries to own so many colonies.

Sometimes, these countries would not let American merchants trade in their colonies.

In the 1890s, Spain owned some islands in the Pacific Ocean and in the Caribbean Sea. The Philippines and Guam were Spanish colonies in the Pacific Ocean. These colonies were far from the United States. Cuba and Puerto Rico were Spanish colonies in the Caribbean Sea. These colonies were near the east coast of the United States.

In the 1890s, American companies bought a lot of sugar cane from Cuba. They made sugar from this sugar cane and sold it to people in the United States. The companies did not have to pay taxes on this import. But in 1894, Congress made a law. It said that merchants had to pay a high tax on this import. American companies did not want to pay this tax. So they did not buy so much sugar cane from Cuba. Many people in Cuba lost their jobs.

In 1895, the people in Cuba fought a revolution against Spain. The Cubans did not want their country to be a colony anymore. The revolution stopped the trade between the United States and Cuba. Some Americans owned companies in Cuba. They did not want Cuba to fight a revolution.

Some Americans wanted the United States to own Cuba. Other Americans wanted Cuba to have its independence. Most Americans did not want the Spanish navy in the Caribbean Sea. In 1897, President McKinley said that the United States would not help in this war.

In February 1898, some people blew up an American ship in Cuba. Many Americans died on this ship. Then more Americans said that the United States should fight a war against Spain.

President McKinley still did not want the United States to fight a war. He sent some men to Spain. Spain said that the Cubans could have their own government. But Cuba would still be a Spanish colony.

By April 1898, many more Americans wanted to fight a war against Spain. President McKinley and Congress decided that the United States would fight against Spain. President McKinley sent the navy to Cuba. The navy helped Cuba to fight for its independence. The American navy also fought against the Spanish navy in the Philippines.

American soldiers fought against Spanish soldiers in Cuba.

Spain and the United States did not fight very long. In December 1898, these countries wrote a treaty. It said that Spain did not own Cuba anymore. Cuba would start its own government. Spain had to give Puerto Rico and Guam to the United States. The United States would buy the Philippines.

Americans did not know what to do with these islands. Many Americans did not want the United States to own colonies. Some Americans thought that the United States could use these islands in wars. Some Americans thought that they could trade with the people on these islands.

After 1898, the United States made rules for the governments of these islands. Sometimes, Congress let these governments make all their own laws. Other times, Congress made special laws for these islands. The governments of these islands had to make the people obey these laws. Sometimes, the American army fought against the people in these islands.

Hawaii

Hawaii is in the Pacific Ocean. After 1865, many Americans started companies in Hawaii. These companies grew sugar cane and pineapple. They sold these things in the United States. The United States and Hawaii wrote treaties. Some of these treaties said that only American companies could trade in Hawaii. Part of the American navy could live in Hawaii.

In 1893, some people in Hawaii did not want American companies or the navy to be in Hawaii anymore. The queen of Hawaii told the American companies and the American navy to leave Hawaii. But other people in Hawaii wanted Hawaii to be part of the United States. These people traded with American companies. The people in Hawaii started to fight. They did not fight very long.

Some people in Hawaii started a new government. This government wanted American companies to stay in Hawaii. It also wanted Hawaii to be part of the United States. The United States talked to this government about Hawaii. It did not talk to the queen.

Congress talked about Hawaii for a long time. Some members of Congress thought that Hawaii should become a territory of the United States. Other members thought that Hawaii should have its own government. Hawaii became a territory of the United States in 1898.

China

China and Japan are countries in Asia. China has a lot of land and raw materials. In 1894, Japan wanted more land and raw materials. So it started a war against China. In 1895, the war was over. Japan took over a small part of China.

After the war, China was not so strong anymore. So Russia, Japan, and some European countries tried to take over different parts of China. Each country said that other countries could not trade in their part of China. The United States was afraid that Americans would not be able to trade with China anymore.

In 1899, the United States sent a letter to Russia, Japan, and some European countries. This letter talked about trade with China. The United States would make sure that all countries could trade in China. It would also make sure that the government of China could get its taxes on imports. All countries would have to pay the same prices to use the railroads and ports in China.

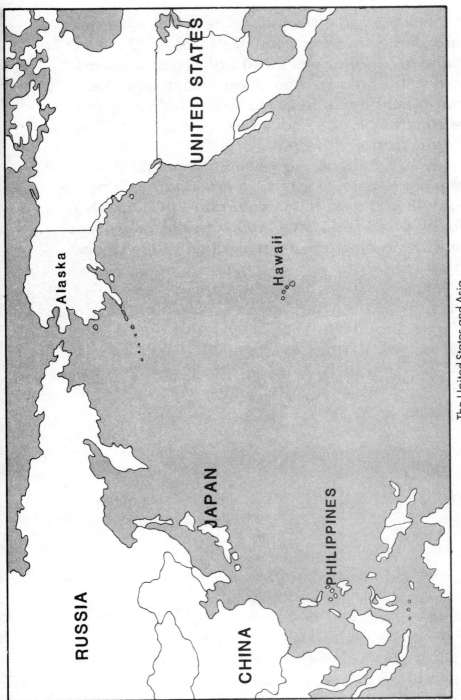

The United States and Asia

In 1900, some people in China did not want the merchants from other countries to be in China anymore. So they started to fight against these merchants. Soldiers from these countries came to fight against the people in China. They helped the merchants from their countries. The United States sent its army to stop this fight.

After this fight, the United States said that it did not want any country to own any part of China. All countries could trade in every part of China. No country could keep other countries out of a part of China. The other countries listened to the United States.

CHAPTER 12

The Presidents: 1896-1912

President McKinley

In 1897, McKinley became the president. In 1898, Americans fought in the Spanish-American War. After this war, the United States owned more territories in the world.

President Theodore Roosevelt

In 1900, Americans had to vote for the next president. The Republicans wanted President McKinley to be president for four more years. The Democrats wanted William Jennings Bryan to be the next president. Americans voted. McKinley became the president again.

In 1901, someone killed President McKinley. Theodore Roosevelt was the vice president. He became president.

President Theodore Roosevelt

President Roosevelt knew that American people and companies had not taken good care of some land. When the land was not good anymore, they moved away. President Roosevelt wanted the federal government to own some land in a special way. The government would take good care of this land. Some of this land became parks. No one could own this land. But anyone could go to see it.

President Theodore Roosevelt and John Muir looked at land in California.

President Roosevelt wanted to help the farmers. Some land in the United States was very dry. So Congress made a law about this land. The law said that the government would help to bring water to this land. Then it would be better for farmers.

In 1902, a union of coal miners went on strike. Railroad companies owned the coal mines. The miners wanted more money and safer mines. They also wanted to work for only nine hours a day. They wanted the railroad companies to talk to their union.

The miners were on strike for a long time. People needed coal to heat their houses. Factories needed coal to make electricity. Then their machines could work. The owners of the mines wanted President Roosevelt to send the army. It would get the coal out of the mines.

President Roosevelt did not want the strike to go on any longer. But he did not want to send the army to the mines. So he sent a group of men to end the strike. They listened to the miners and the owners. Then they decided what to do. The miners would get more money. They would only have to work for nine hours a day. But the owners would not have to talk to the union.

Some people were very angry. They knew that the government could take some big companies to court. They wanted the federal government to use the federal law against all big companies. But the government did not take many big companies to court.

In 1903, President Roosevelt decided that the federal government should use this law more often. So he told the court to take some big companies to court. The court said that these big companies had to become many smaller companies again. But these small companies still got together and talked about prices. Then they could still get high prices for their things.

The ICC said that railroad companies had to let everyone pay the same price for the same trip. But the railroad companies wanted the big companies to use their railroad. So they gave money back to some big companies. Then these companies still paid less money to use the railroads. Small companies and farmers still had to pay more money than big companies. In 1903, Congress made another law about railroads. It said that the railroad companies could not give money back to big companies.

In 1904, Americans had to vote for the next president. The Republicans wanted President Roosevelt to be president for four more years. The Democrats wanted Alton Parker to be the next president. Some Americans were members of another party. This party was the Socialist Party. This party wanted the government to own some kinds of companies. Then people would not have to pay so much money for some things. The Socialists wanted Eugene Debs to be the next president.

Americans voted. Theodore Roosevelt was the president for four more years.

In 1906, Congress made another law about railroad companies. This law gave more power to the ICC. It could make more rules for railroad companies.

In 1906, Congress made a law about foods in cans. This law started a new group in the federal government. This group could make rules about food companies. These rules say that foods in cans must be safe to eat.

In 1906, Congress also made a law about meat. The law said that people from the government had to look at meat. They had to say if the meat was safe to eat. Then people could sell this meat to people in another state.

In 1906, Congress changed the law about the land of the first Americans. This new law said that first Americans could sell their land on the reservations. Then many first Americans sold their land. They moved to cities. This law also said that these first Americans could vote. But the first Americans on reservations could not vote.

Before 1906, only first Americans lived in the special territory for first Americans. There were many reservations in this territory. After 1906, many first Americans sold some of the land on these reservations. Then Americans owned some of this land. By 1907, many Americans lived in this territory. It was called Oklahoma. They wanted Oklahoma to become a state. In 1907, Oklahoma became a state.

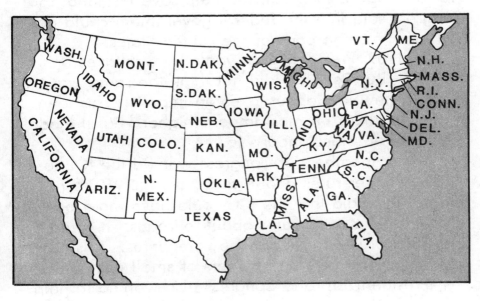

The United States in 1907

In 1908, Americans had to vote for the next president. Many people wanted President Roosevelt to be president for four more years. But President Roosevelt said that a man should not be president for more than eight years. So the Republicans wanted William Howard Taft to be the next president. The Democrats wanted William Jennings Bryan to be the next president.

The AFL also wanted Bryan to be the next president. They told workers in their unions to vote for Bryan. Americans voted. Taft became the next president.

President Taft

President Taft also wanted to help many people and small companies. So the federal government took more big companies to court. The courts made some big companies become lots of smaller companies. President Taft also wanted to help save the land. So Congress said that the federal government could not sell land in some parts of the United States.

In 1909, President Taft wanted lower taxes on imports. But Congress did not think the same way. It made a new law about taxes on imports. This law made the taxes on most imports higher. But it made the taxes on other imports lower.

Many members of Congress wanted the ICC to make stronger rules about railroads. In 1910, a new federal law said that the ICC could have more power. It could make more rules about railroads. It could also make rules for telephone companies. This new law helped farmers and owners of small companies.

President Taft and Congress also wanted to help workers. They made a law about workers in some kinds of companies. These companies did some work for the federal government. The law said that these workers had to work for only eight hours a day.

In 1912, many Americans lived in the New Mexico Territory. These Americans wanted their land to become states. Congress said that their land could become the states of Arizona and New Mexico.

In 1912, Americans had to vote for the next president. Theodore Roosevelt did not think that President Taft had been a good president. Roosevelt thought that he had been a good president for eight years. So he wanted to be president again. Some Republicans also wanted Roosevelt to be president. Other Republicans wanted President Taft to be president for four more years. The Democrats wanted Woodrow Wilson to be the next president. Americans voted. Wilson became the next president.

President Wilson

Many members of Congress thought that the government needed more money. They wanted to make a law about taxes on income. But the Supreme Court had said that the old law about taxes on income was against the Constitution. So Congress wrote an amendment to the Constitution. The 16th Amendment says that the government can make laws about taxes on income.

Many Americans wanted to vote for senators in Congress. They did not think that the representatives in the state governments should vote for these senators. So Congress made another amendment to the Constitution. The 17th Amendment says that Americans can vote for their senators in Congress. In 1913, the 16th and 17th Amendments became part of the Constitution.

In 1913, Congress made a law about taxes. It made taxes on many imports lower. This law also said that some Americans and companies had to pay taxes on their incomes. Richer Americans had to pay more taxes on their incomes than other Americans.

President Wilson had to think about the banks. There were no federal banks. Many Americans wanted to change the banks in the United States. They wanted big banks to help other banks. Some Americans wanted big companies to own the big banks. Other Americans wanted the federal government to take care of the big banks.

In 1913, Congress made a law about banks. This law started 12 federal banks. People and companies could not use these banks. These federal banks would help other banks. If a bank had trouble, it could borrow money from these federal banks. The law also made a new group in the federal government. This group would make rules for banks in the United States.

President Wilson thought that some companies were too big. He wanted Congress to make stronger laws against big companies. In 1914, Congress made a new law about big companies. It said that big companies had to have the same prices for everybody. A big company could not make small companies buy things from it. Companies could buy things from many other companies. Sometimes, many small companies did the same kind of work. A big company could not own all of these small companies.

This law helped farmers and workers. It also said that workers could have unions. Unions could go on strike. Farmers could work together in the Grange.

In 1914, Congress started a special group. It

makes rules for some kinds of big companies. These companies work in many states. The rules say that these companies have to be fair. The group can make the companies obey its rules. It can take them to court.

In 1916, Congress made a law about money for farmers. This law said that special banks could let farmers borrow money. The farmers would not have to pay a lot of extra money to the banks for this money.

Many European countries had been fighting a war for two years. President Wilson had kept the United States out of this war. Many Americans were glad. They did not want to fight in this war.

In 1916, Americans had to vote for the next president. The Democrats wanted President Wilson to be president for four more years. The Republicans wanted Charles Evans Hughes to be the next president. Americans voted. President Wilson became the president for the next four years.

CHAPTER 13

The United States and the Americas

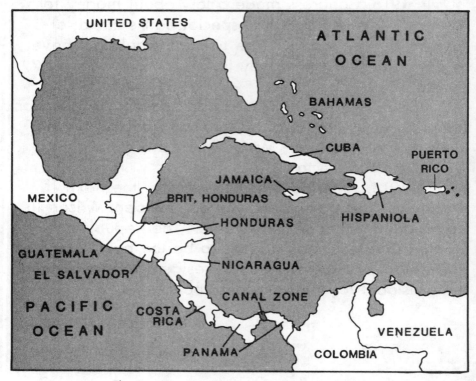

The Panama Canal and the Caribbean Islands

The Caribbean Islands

After the Spanish-American War, the presidents of the United States had to think more about the world. The United States owned some islands in the Caribbean Sea and the Pacific Ocean. It also owned Alaska. Each president had to think about the people in these American lands. Some Americans wanted these people to become Americans. Other Americans wanted them to have their own countries. Other Americans did not want the United States to change the government of these people.

In 1900, the United States owned Puerto Rico. Congress made a law about the government of Puerto Rico. This law said that Americans could help to make the laws for Puerto Rico. Many people in Puerto Rico did not like this law. They wanted to have more power in their own government. In 1917, Puerto Rico became an American territory. Then people in Puerto Rico could have their own government. But the laws of this government could not go against the federal laws and the Constitution.

After the Spanish-American War, Spain did not own Cuba anymore. But Cuba did not have its own government. The American army and navy were still in Cuba. In 1901, Congress made a law about Cuba. It said that the Cubans could have their own government. But the United States could help change this government. Cuba could not make treaties with other countries. It had to let the United States keep its navy in Cuba.

Some Cubans did not want American companies in Cuba. Sometimes, they fought against these companies. Between 1906 and 1920, Congress sent American soldiers to Cuba three times. The soldiers helped the American companies.

Panama

In the early 1900s, the United States owned islands in the Pacific Ocean and in the Caribbean Sea. If there was trouble in these places, the United States could not send soldiers quickly. There were no airplanes. The navy had to go around South America.

Americans wanted the United States to build a canal in Central America. Then the navy and other ships could travel faster between the Atlantic and Pacific oceans. These trips also would not cost so much money.

Panama and Colombia are in Central America. Some Americans thought that the canal should be in Panama. The government of Colombia owned Panama. The United States talked to the government of Colombia. In 1903, they wrote a treaty. It said that the United States would pay money for some land in Panama. Congress liked this treaty. But the government of Colombia did not like it. So the United States could not build the canal yet.

The people in Panama wanted the canal in Panama. But they did not want their land to be part of Colombia. They wanted their own government. So they fought against the government of Colombia. The United States helped the people in Panama. Then Panama won its revolution.

Americans dug the Panama Canal.

In 1904, the United States made a treaty with Panama. It said that the United States would pay money to Panama. Every year, it would pay rent for some land. The United States could build the canal on this land. In 1914, the canal was ready. Then boats could use this canal.

The government of Colombia was angry at the United States for many years. Columbia said that the United States should not have helped Panama in its revolution. In 1921, the United States paid some money to Colombia. Then Colombia was not so angry anymore.

Europe and the Americas

In 1823, President Monroe had said that the United States would help the countries in Central America and South America. The United States would not let European countries make any more colonies there.

But many countries in Central America and South America were not very strong. Sometimes, they borrowed money from European countries and could not pay it back. Then the European countries said that they would try to take over these countries in Central America and South America. But these countries did not want the European countries to take over their governments. Sometimes, the United States talked to the European countries. It did not want these countries to fight against each other.

In 1904, President Roosevelt said that the United States would give more help to the countries in Central America and South America. The American army would help these countries to fight against the European countries. Then the European countries could not take their land.

After 1904, the United States helped some countries in Central and South America. It talked to some American banks. These banks let some governments in Central and South America borrow money. Then these countries could pay back the money to the European countries. But these countries could not always pay back the money to the American banks. Then American bankers and the army went to these countries. They tried to tell these governments what to do. But the people did not want the United States to take over their governments.

Mexico

Between 1910 and 1914, the government of Mexico changed a few times. These governments were not very strong. Some Americans owned land and companies in Mexico. They were afraid that the Mexicans would take over American land and companies in Mexico.

In 1914, many Americans wanted President Wilson to send the army to Mexico. But he thought that the Mexicans would make a new government very soon. He thought that this government would help the Americans. So he did not send the army.

In 1914, a man from the Mexican government took some American sailors off their ship. President Wilson was angry. So he sent the navy to Mexico. Then three countries in South America decided to meet with Mexico and the United States. They did not want Mexico and the United States to fight. After this meeting, Mexico had a new president. The American navy left Mexico. The new Mexican government said that Americans could keep their land and companies in Mexico.

Some Mexicans did not want American companies in Mexico. So they killed some Americans. President Wilson got angry. He sent the army to Mexico. The army tried to help Americans and their companies. But in 1917, the American army left Mexico. The American army had to fight in Europe.